THIS BOOK IS DEDICATED TO THE PEOPLE WHO HELPED CREATE AND CHANGE MY STORY...

Michael Gerber: *for his loving friendship and The Dreaming Room challenge to "Find what is impossible and then go do it."*

My wife: *Paula, for being all that I love.*

My children: *Don, Jr., Anne, Lauren, and Meredith, for keeping me young.*

My patients: *Who shared the stories of their lives.*

5 a.m.

& Already
Behind

DR. DON KENNEDY, MBA

Foreword by **Michael E. Gerber**
New York Times Best-Selling Author

NEW YORK

5 a.m. & Already Behind

By Dr. Don Kennedy, MBA

© 2008 Don Kennedy. All rights reserved.

ISBN: 978-1-60037-344-2   Paperback

Published by:

MORGAN · JAMES
THE ENTREPRENEURIAL PUBLISHER™

Morgan James Publishing, LLC
1225 Franklin Ave Ste 325
Garden City, NY 11530-1693
Toll Free 800-485-4943
www.MorganJamesPublishing.com

Cover and Interior Design by:

Heather Kirk
www.GraphicsByHeather.com
Heather@GraphicsByHeather.com

Habitat for Humanity®
Peninsula
Building Partner

READERS ARE RAVING...

"As a business owner, I was struggling to find that balance between work, health and family. There simply were not enough hours in the day for me until I read this book."

Scott Jackson, Partner, EVOK Advertising

"Read this book with the knowledge that the man who wrote it did so because he has seen the price his patients have paid for not paying attention to what he has shared with us here and have paid a dear price for it."

Michael E. Gerber, Author of The E-Myth Books And Chief Dreamer in The Dreaming Room

"Dr. Kennedy leverages a 20+ year career in medicine and interviewing those at the end of their life to discover what holds you back from having what you want today. By discovering just one Bahbit, I was able to lose 45 pounds in just over three months!"

Dave Lakhani, President, Bold Approach, Inc

"Dr. Don provides the tools to nail the hang ups and identify the clutter we all have that lurks below the surface,

sabotaging our goals, dreams and the life we all desire. Do yourself a favor — begin the journey of applying these tools today — your future may depend on it."

Guy Allen, Financial Specialist

"Who wants to grow old and have to live with a bunch of regrets? If you follow what Dr. Don says you can live the life you were meant to live. This is a must read if you want to change your life."

Dallas Shepard, Area Director, Young Life International

"Become involved and Dr. Kennedy will focus your thoughts toward a healthier and more meaningful existence."

Jon Williams, C.S.C.S, Exercise Physiologist,
Wellness Director

"So compelling in its exploration, a daring assessment of self discovery; learn what is limiting your potential."

Darcie Allen, Professional Fitness Instructor,
Professional/Musician

FOREWORD

By Michael E. Gerber
Author of *The E-Myth Books*
And Chief Dreamer in The Dreaming Room

I love small books! I guess the older I get, the less patient I get with people who simply go on and on about Nothing hoping to turn it into Something.

This delightful little book is about Something. And Dr. Don (my affectionate name for the author) has eloquently and directly communicated a little secret each and every one of us will benefit from to the degree we feel out of control and are determined to do something about it.

Read this book with the knowledge that the man who wrote it did so because he has seen the price his patients have paid for not paying attention to what he has shared with us here and have paid a dear price for it.

Dr. Don is determined that for the rest of his life he will remind all of us that life is short, and that living is rich, and that we each deserve the very best we can get.

This is the first of his wonderfully short and elegant books to keep that promise to you, his reader.

Just read it!

I KNOW YOU

It's late. It's the end of your life, and I've heard your story a million times. This book is about now, not later. It will teach you how to change the course of your life to a story of love and health and success. Follow Mike; he's no different than you.

~*Dr. D.E. Kennedy*

TABLE OF CONTENTS

TO HELP YOU ON YOUR JOURNEY TO SUCCESS...

At the end of many of the chapters throughout this book, you will find assignments, which will help you on your journey to finding love and health and success now. I highly recommend that you download this free bonus workbook to compliment each of the assignments.

You can download the free PDF at a special page on our website:

www.Its5am.com/bonusworkbook

Get your free PDF today and best wishes for finding the best in life now.

~Dr. D.E. Kennedy

CHAPTER 1
Meet Mike

CHAPTER 1
Meet Mike

It's 5 AM; Mike is already behind. The clock has too many buttons. As he does most mornings, he gropes, gives up, and twists the volume control. It's quiet again.

He stares into the dark without thoughts; he's tired. He listens to his wife's dream-breathing and wants to shut his eyes — just a few minutes. There are only two times during the work week: now and late.

Sitting up, he wiggles his toes. "Here we go," he whispers and stands, arms limp. It's too early to move. The closet light minimizes reality as he shuffles toward the bathroom.

He hangs at the sink listening to the shower and asks his subconscious to think through the next ten hours. There is no catching up, only survival. As most mornings, he wishes for Saturday. "I just want to get through this day," he thinks, and tries to remember how many times he'd had that thought. "How about every morning," he mumbles and steps into the steam.

In the hint of sunrise, Mike aims his car for the office twenty miles away. He stops for a drive-thru coffee and arrives twenty minutes early. "I'm out of shape and too fat," he thinks as he catches his breath half way up the steps. "This weekend I'm going to start walking."

Mike is surprised, the office is lit; he smells fresh coffee. Reaching his cubicle, he hears a noise on the far side of the maze. Tiptoeing, he peeks in to see Ben flipping through an open folder, one hand on his hip.

"Hey Ben..."

Ben jerks.

"Sorry, I thought you heard me come in."

"That's O.K., I was just double checking this project before Mr. Big goes through it."

"Is that the Smoker Project?"

"Yes it is." Ben drops the folder into a wire basket marked "Complete".

"I thought he gave you a couple months to finish that."

"He did." Ben looks at Mike. "But, I wanted to stay caught up with everything; I sleep better."

"You mean you're all caught up...on everything, right now?" Mike squints at the closed folder.

5 a.m. & Already Behind

"That's my new mantra, get it done and keep everything caught up by the end of the day."

Ben is calm and eases into his swivel chair.

Mike is speechless; making a subtle bow he turns and ambles toward the coffee room. He's anxious, but why? He stops and half turns, loses a thought, and mumbles, "You've got to be kidding me." Rubbing his tongue inside his cheek, he thinks, "I know he's got just as much work as I do; probably more. How is he caught up and I'm smothered?" Sitting in his cubicle he stares at the fuzzy tan walls and tries to figure it out. It bugs him all day.

It's 5:15 PM and Mike lingers at the water fountain timing his entrance to the elevator. He steps in behind Ben.

"What a day," Mike sighs and looks down. "What's in the bag?"

"My gym stuff, it's racquetball day."

Mike is drained; Ben isn't tired. "This is crazy," Mike thinks and gazes at the elevator light. He drives home thinking about Ben and work and tomorrow.

That next morning Mike arrives thirty minutes early, Ben is at his desk. "You have got to be kidding me," Mike whispers and peeks over his cubicle wall. "He's got to be on something."

Mike snorts as he eases across the office. He doesn't know Ben well, they started two years ago. "This guy was never a star," he mutters, "he looks different, no, he acts different. Something's different." Mike announces himself with a cough.

"I hear you this time, Mike. Man, you're early. Did you get that Benson case finished?"

"No, I was on it until almost midnight but fell asleep. The nights are too short."

"Yeah, that's the way it used to be for me."

The question door opened. "What do you mean 'it used to be' like that?"

Ben swiveled and looked up. "Let's just say I had to make some changes."

"Tell me, what changes?"

"I was tired of life, but I met a man who helped me figure it out."

"What man?" Mike was direct. "Look Ben, I'm tired and I'm behind and I'm gonna die if I don't lose some weight. You come in here early, you've got everything done, and you don't look tired. What gives?"

"He's sort of a coach, a personal coach, and he shows people how to make changes so they can quit living the never-ending day. I'm done with that," Ben was serious.

They stared. Mike let the silence ask the question.

"Hey, it's not easy, but if you want, I'll give him your number."

"What's his name?" Mike wrote on a yellow pad.

"Guy..." Ben put the paper in his top pocket, "I'll ask him to call you this week."

CHAPTER 2
Clutter

CHAPTER 2
Clutter

The odor of garlic and Italian bread made Mike tug his coat as he entered the empty Italian restaurant. He was greeted by a pudgy chef dressed in black slacks and half open shirt wiping his hands on a waist apron.

"Benvenuto, you must be Mr. Lamb?" The accent was authentic. Mike nodded as the man pressed Mike's arm and motioned, "Guy is at the back table, please let me take you to him."

Guy sat at corner table. He was lanky and well-groomed with slight graying and an air of wisdom. As Mike approached, Guy stood and extended his hand, his grip was confident. Mike liked him.

"I'm Guy Brussard." Half gesturing toward the other tables, "Is this O.K. for our meeting?"

"Oh yeah," Mike looked back at the red tablecloths. "This smells a lot better than my office."

"I try to meet in different places, it gives my clients and me a chance to see other parts of the city and get us out of our usual pace."

I love new places," Mike sat and held up two fingers. "I have two places I visit: home and work. This is great."

They sat facing each other as Guy thanked the waiter and gestured for a refill of coffee; Mike did the same.

"How long have you known Ben?"

"We joined the firm two years ago but never met before that. Honestly, we've worked on some project teams together and we talk, but we're not close friends."

"But you know him well enough to see something is different about him?"

"Yeah, that's really what led to this meeting. He's changed, but I couldn't figure out what exactly it was that did change. I know he's lost weight, but there's something else. For some reason he's more noticeable, maybe he's happier. All of a sudden Ben's one of the best employees we have. If something needs to be done, he's the one everybody wants on their team. And, the bosses know it."

"And you?" Guy leaned back as the waiter poured coffee. "Why do you think we're here?"

5 a.m. & Already Behind

"I'm not sure. I saw Ben and looked at my life and just got frustrated. We do about the same thing, but he's off playing racquetball and way ahead on everything while I'm looking at the clock wondering where the time went. Maybe I'm just not happy with myself." He stopped and looked into his coffee. "I guess I thought I'd be doing better than I am." Shrugging, he looked at Guy. "I just don't know, I really just don't know."

"It sounds like you need a little help to think through some things; you're a lot like Ben, ambitious but unfocused. That's where I helped him and I think I can help you... if that's all right?"

Ben sipped his coffee, nodded, and folded his hands on the table.

"If you're wondering what I do; I'm a coach, you can call me a life coach." Guy paused and placed a black leather notebook on the table, it was bound with a gold paper seal. "I help people learn to focus on what's important and enjoy, rather than run through, their lives. If you want change, all you have to do is follow a few rules...if that's all right with you?"

Ben thought about rules. What rules? His throat was tight and he felt flushed. Guy read the emotion.

"You feel uncomfortable, right?" Ben looked across the restaurant as Guy leaned closer. "Mike, the rules are simple and most people actually enjoy the process."

"O.K., what are the rules?"

"The first rule is about our meetings. I'm going to give you a new assignment out of this workbook every two weeks and we'll go over it at our meetings. I'm not saying it's easy, but it's doable. It's how it all starts. I've done this program with hundreds of clients. You'll see how it works just by doing it. It's not painful, in a physical sense, but it does take time, time you don't think you have.

Guy slid the notebook across the table, Ben read the gold embossing: "Clutter."

"I can do that, what else?" He looked up.

"Just two more rules: you must make all the meetings, no excuses, and be at least ten minutes early. Ben, I know it might sound silly but it's important. I can help you straighten things out, but I'm strict with the rules. What do you think?"

"That's it?" Mike was relieved.

"Well, there's a lot more to it; those are just the rules."

"OK, I'm in, what happens now?" Mike dropped his shoulders and sat back.

5 a.m. & Already Behind

"Clutter," Guy's tone was definitive. "Your first assignment is about clutter. Here's what you do."

Ben leaned forward as Guy flipped to the first page.

"When you get home you'll open the workbook to Chapter One, here. The pages are pretty much blank except for the headings on each page. As you can see, each page is broken down into different times over the next year. Your first assignment starts tomorrow, not the day after.

Ben cringed and repeated, "Tomorrow."

"You're going to write down all the things you think you have to do in all the areas of your life. Mike, notice the book has some areas that are common to all of us, but I've left room for you to be a little creative; we're all different. If there's one area you'd like to add, please do so."

"Is that it?" Mike closed the notebook.

"That's it for the first assignment; there is one other thing" Guy raised his index finger. "You'll notice there are several sections in the notebook. At each of our meetings I'll give you one assignment; please don't read or work ahead. I want you to concentrate only on the assignment I give you. Is that fair?"

"Got it..."

"I'll call you this week and let you know where we're meeting next."

They stood and shook hands. Mike was playful, "Thanks Guy, this should be fun; I hope I have enough time."

ASSIGNMENT NUMBER ONE

1 Find a quiet place and a time that will allow you to work on your assignments for at least *fifteen minutes* or more each day. There may be *times* you have to change, but in order for the assignment to be effective, you *must do it daily.*

2 The first assignment is to identify the clutter in your life; all the things that take up your time. These are the things you're constantly thinking and worrying about that may be sapping your energy and limiting your ability to focus on what you really need to be doing.

3 In your bonus downloadable PDF workbook, start with the page marked "Today" and write all the tasks you have to do, or think you have to do, in the four general areas of your life. When that is completed, add other areas that are unique to you. General areas are listed in the notebook include: family, work, finances, and health and fitness. You might want to add more specific areas like church or clubs, those specific to your lifestyle and unique to you.

4 Once you've written those for *today*, move onto the week and month and finish with the year. Use the same areas as those you wrote for "Today". You'll note that as you move toward the year, your task list becomes less in number and more general in nature.

5 Once you've completed the assignment on the first day, take time over the next few days or weeks to refine your list. Put a line thorough the items you complete and add new items if needed. It's important to *date* both the items completed and the new items added.

CHAPTER 3
Habits

CHAPTER 3
Habits

Mike slouched beneath a dripping umbrella on Saturday morning. The city was hazy. "I haven't been in a library in twenty years," he thought as he climbed long steps through a revolving door. The library was musty. He relaxed and wasn't sure why.

Guy was talking to a woman in her sixties wearing a blue blazer. Her posture was straight and she was laughing. They turned and smiled as Mike approached.

"Your fifteen minutes early." Guy looked at his watch.

"You told me to follow the rules."

"Hey, discipline is the first criteria."

"Mike, this is a great friend of mine, Linda."

Linda placed her glasses on the counter and extended her hand, "So, you're the victim today."

"Yes, I guess I am." Her grasp matched her directness.

"Linda is the chief librarian; I've known her for several years." Guy winked at Linda then gestured toward the shelves of books, "She's trying to read every book in this place."

"No Guy, I've already read all nine hundred thousand; I'm just starting my second time through." She glanced at Mike. "I have a special room for you and Guy," pointing to the escalator, "the fun begins on the second floor. Oh, and Mike," placing a finger near her lips, "please be quiet, it's a problem Guy has around here."

From the escalator Mike saw his elementary school library and first grade teacher, Mrs. Penny. "When was the last time I had time to read a book," he thought as Guy motioned toward an open door.

The room was sparse; one frayed couch, a recliner, and a table with four chairs in the center. The glow from a table lamp mixed with sunlight from a high window accented dusty encyclopedias. It felt like a living room.

"What do you think of this library?"

"It's been a long time; they all smell the same." Mike pulled his workbook from a briefcase and placed it on the table. They sat down, Mike felt awkward.

"How did these past two weeks go?"

Mike tapped the workbook and looked past Guy. "It was busy; I didn't get a lot of sleep."

"Why do you think you had trouble sleeping?"

"The usual. All the stuff I've written in this workbook, it weighs ten pounds."

Guy appreciated Mike's humor. "How did it feel to write it down?"

"Actually...it felt good. Once I got rolling, I couldn't stop. No wonder I'm drowning." Mike shuffled the pages then stopped.

"Let's talk about your clutter, would that be O.K.?

"Absolutely..."

"Clutter, all the things you've written, is the reason most people can't get through their day. A cluttered day leads to a cluttered and frustrating life. You can write and plan and review your life's goals every day, but like most people, you'll end up with just a 'list of hopes'. Like them, you'll spend your daylight struggling to get a handle on the unwritten list, the 'get done first' list."

Guy studied Mike's face. "Who's buried under the clutter? It's you, the real Mike, the Mike with passion and purpose; the Mike that used to play and create and dream. That's where that Mike lives."

Mike pictured sunrise lighting a yellow mountain of sticky notes.

"Mike," Guy's tone was softer. "Why do you think you have four pages of 'tasks', things to do?"

Mike thumbed the pages then shook his head. "I don't know, this stuff seems important, but you're right, I never get it done." He paused and repeated, "Just never get it done."

"I want you to finish every task in this assignment by tomorrow."

Mike was startled. "What…?"

"Just kidding, take it easy." He patted Mike's arm. "But, just think, if you were tied to a timeline and had to finish everything you've written this week, which one would you do first?"

Mike licked his lips.

"You'd be forced to prioritize, right?" Guy's voice was slow and deliberate. "Why do have this huge list?"

"I just don't know; I guess I've always had a list." Mike tapped the page.

5 a.m. & Already Behind

"That a great answer and that takes us to next week's assignment."

Mike's was disappointed.

"Listen Mike, you'll see how this pulls together. Just promise you'll do the assignments and follow the rules."

"I know... I'm always in a hurry."

"Think of all those books." Guy gestured toward the library, "How do you think all these authors found time to write and create and learn?"

"Good question."

"That's our next assignment; these authors had the discipline to create a miracle. They understood priorities and developed habits to support the discipline to get things done." Guy stopped with an up-tone in his voice, "But that's for our session in two weeks."

Mike studied the ceiling, hands laced across his chest.

"Over the next two weeks I'd like you to go to Assignment Two in your workbook and list all your habits — the very actions, or inactions, which shape your day, your week and your life. Notice, like the first chapter, the pages are divided into the same general areas. Remember to add the same unique areas you added in the first assignment.

Mike sat forward and studied the workbook.

"Each area is divided into three columns labeled for your habits: good, bad, and should.

Mike smirked, "Now this should be interesting."

"You'll notice as you progress through time that some of your habits are redundant. That's O.K, that's what habits do.

Mike thought of his toothbrush.

"Take your time and try to notice how each day goes. Ask yourself 'what's the same,' and note how your habits change on your days off." He paused, "What are you thinking?"

"This is scary."

"A little anxious..?"

"Oh yeah... this is going to be a reality check, but I know it's got to be done."

"Mike, my friend," Guy closed the workbook, his voice low. "Most people live lifetimes without a reality check."

ASSIGNMENT NUMBER TWO

1 Using chapter two in the bonus workbook, or on a blank piece of paper, make a list of the four areas as you did in chapter one: *Work, family, health and fitness, and finance.* Then add any unique areas you may have added in chapter one.

2 Make a grid by dividing the paper into three columns each separated by areas you have listed. At the top of each column write: *Good, Bad and Should.*

- **Good Habits**: Are those that you do regularly improve your life

- **Bad Habits**: Are those that you do frequently and detract from your life

- **Should Habits**: Are those you know you should be doing, but don't.

3 In each of the areas under *good, bad, and should* write habits that you feel correspond to that particular area of your life and also fall under the horizontal headings.

(Some examples could be sleeping too late or getting easily angered). It is normal to have the same habit, or lack of habit, appear in several different areas.

4 Over two weeks refine these areas as you go through your day. You may find you need to add more but *do not remove any already written*.

5 If a habit is specific for a weekend, or a day away from your usual workday, note that day (*weekend or holiday*) next to the habit.

CHAPTER 4

A Walk Thorough Your Life

30

CHAPTER 4
A Walk Thorough Your Life

"Trains are fascinating," Mike thought as he inspected the stained block of the old station. The icon was still active as a major hub, and its renovation had revitalized the central city.

The elevator opened into an upscale restaurant that overlooked the passenger terminal through soundproof glass. Mike stepped out then ambled over to Guy who was talking to a tall man in a baggy, grey stripped uniform.

Guy was excited. "Hey Mike, isn't this place incredible?"

Mike surveyed the trains and people.

"It's hard to believe that we're looking at an organized system."

Mike remained quiet.

"But, somehow it all works." Guy finished as the engineer stepped forward and bent toward Mike.

"Hi Mike...I'm Harry."

Harry had deep smile lines and stark blue eyes. Mike guessed he was fifty years old.

"I get to run one of those babies down there." Harry thumbed toward the trains.

"Hey, that sounds better than my job."

"Oh, believe me, it is, and I get to do it every day."

"And he gets dirty and sweats," Guy interrupted.

Harry's smile lines deepened, "And some people are shiny and clean and jealous."

"And those things are true," Guy turned to Mike. "I keep threatening to go down there and take one for a ride."

"That reminds me, I really do have a train to catch. Mike, it was great meeting you, just please... keep Guy up here and away from anything mechanical."

"Thanks Harry," Mike searched Guy. "I'm sensing he has a reputation everywhere he goes."

They watched Harry swagger as Mike marveled at the history of locomotives told through black and white murals adorning the steep walls.

"I had a train set when I was a kid," Mike said passively as he sat and stretched his legs. "I bet shoveling coal was a lot harder than what I do."

5 a.m. & Already Behind

"Mike, tell me about the past couple weeks; did you discover anything?" Guy was relaxed; his tone expectant.

"Habits I am; I am a bag of habits. My wife called them quirks."

"What do you mean?"

"My life is built like an Egyptian pyramid. Instead of those massive blocks of stone, it's built with huge habits. I'm completely dependent on those stone-habits to keep everything from collapsing."

"I've never heard that analogy before."

"I just thought of it."

They laughed as Guy picked up the workbook. "Do you mind?"

Mike shrugged, "No, not really."

"What can you tell me about your good habits?"

Mike tapped his temple. "I can tell you I wished I had more; they were hard to find and the list was short. The longest list was the 'should' habits; I think that's been growing for about twenty years. I should, I should, and I should."

"Were there any bad habits that caught your attention?"

"The usual; I eat too much and don't exercise" He gestured an exclamation point.

"But they all bothered me."

Guy gazed through the glass. "You're right Mike, your habits are the driving force and the building blocks to how you feel and live every diamond moment of your life. There have been a lot of books written about our habits; they drive our lives but most people don't stop to consider why or where they come from. Our habits are like the trains in this old station; habit-trains. People take the first ride for some purpose but eventually forget why they got on in the first place. They ride through their days adding boxcars jammed with clutter.

Mike wondered how many boxcars he was pulling.

Guy slid the notebook to Mike. "Big habits, good or bad, determine the course of our lives. The ugly ones are called 'Bahbits', they crush hope and steal our nights.

"Bahbits...?" Mike's eyes narrowed.

Guy shifted, "Let's talk about your next assignment."

Mike opened the workbook and read, "Chapter Four."

"Chapter Four," Guy repeated. "This assignment is about your life before today. We're going on an expedition to find when and why your bad habits started and which ones you already left behind. You see Mike, to change today you have to understand yesterday. As we go on, you'll see why this Dick Tracy stuff is important."

Mike thought back to college and late nights and calculus.

"You'll notice the pages are divided into decades of your life and there's room to write your thoughts. Put the bad habits you listed in Assignment Two next to the age you think they started. In the column next to that specific habit, try to remember what was going on in your life. Write why they started. Also, list the bad habits you may have already stopped, and why and how you stopped them."

"Pretty simple; let me think about this a little bit."

"That's the idea," Guys voice trailed off. "And please, take the time to do an update of chapter one; see if you've added more clutter."

"Clutter I have; habits I am. Thanks Guy, I'll see you in two weeks."

ASSIGNMENT NUMBER THREE

1 Make a grid with three columns and eight rows.

- Label the first column: *Years*

- Label the second column: *Bad / Changed*

- Label the third column: *Why?*

2 Label the blocks below the first column in increments of ten years:

- Example: 1-10, 10-20, 20-30, etc.

3 Now transfer the bad habits you identified, in assignment number two to the second column and match them with the decade you believe they started.

- These represent the bad habits you continue to carry.

4 In addition, in column two, list and *circle* any bad habits that may have started at some decade in your life and are no longer present.

5 In column three, write what you believe to be the circumstances under which each bad habit was either started or stopped, and why one may continue to this day. You might ask yourself the following:

- Why was going on in my life when I started this bad habit?

- What was the purpose or reason I started it at that time in my life?

- What motivated me to stop a bad habit I started?

- Why do I keep the bad habits I have?

CHAPTER 5
A Walk Through Your Day

40

CHAPTER 5
A Walk Through Your Day

Mike drove past pastures, cows, and long wooden fences as the cool morning blew through open windows. The last time Mike had traveled was a business trip to Los Angeles, hardly the country.

"A cow's life," he thought as he squinted over the steering wheel. Side roads separated squares of green that led over hills to nowhere; they all looked the same.

Guy had emphasized his directions. "Turn right at a little white sign that says 'Betty's'. If you come to a four way stop, you missed it four miles back."

"This is the life," Mike announced. He saw the sign and turned. Bouncing, he pressed the gas and sneered at the dust ball growing in his rear view mirror. Over the hill he turned onto a gravel road leading to a farm house wrapped in a picket porch. Smoke drifted from a black tipped chimney.

Where does he find these places, Mike thought as he pulled into a grass drive way. He stretched then meandered along a path past a sign hung from an L shaped pipe: "Welcome to Betty's."

Guy rocked on the wooden porch next to a square table made from 2 x 4s. Mike clumped up the steps and turned to absorb the view and breeze. Satisfied, he sighed and lowered into a rocker next to Guy. Steam floated as Guy sipped coffee from an irregular mug; neither spoke as they watched a tractor cut a black furrow in a distant square.

"What do you think?"

"I think I wish I were a farmer."

"Do you think you could drive that tractor?"

"You bet. I grew up on a farm kind of like this."

"What was it like to be out there... in all this air?" Guy's chest expanded.

"At first it was great; I tried to be like my dad. But, going back and forth across the field was monotonous. I needed more excitement."

Guy rocked forward as a waitress hummed and poured Mike's coffee. She was thin and striking in a dress and frilled apron, her hands smooth and unblemished. "It looks like Guy was late milking again this morning." She winked at Mike.

5 a.m. & Already Behind

Guy smirked, "It looks like those cows get up way too early for Guy; noon makes a lot more sense."

She placed her hands on her hips in mock disappointment then kissed Guy's forehead, "He's no farmer, but we love him anyway."

"Thanks Betty," Guy grinned and gestured. "Mike says he can drive a tractor."

"Then tomorrow morning, Mike, be here at 4 AM."

"I'll be here," Mike raised his mug. "Just make sure all the Bessies are lined up and full of milk."

She laughed and whirled. The screen door banged as she disappeared.

"O.K. Mike, back to reality," Guy repositioned his rocker. "What can you tell me about the past couple weeks?

Mike opened his workbook and read. "Age eight: bad habit was overeating." He glanced at Guy then back to the workbook. "Because...I was one of the heavy kids in school and my mom always made sure I finished everything, no matter how full I got." He ran his finger down the page. "Oh yeah, I tried the smoking thing at age fourteen but my father fixed that habit before it rooted." Mike's face flushed. "Age 26: spent all my money on a new car and haven't been out of debt since." He thumped the page, slammed the workbook, and grabbed his mug, "Great, Uh?"

"That's pretty serious stuff." Guy let expectation lead the conversation.

"It is funny. My good habits disappeared into should habits and the bad habits planted themselves and kept growing."

"That's what happens to people," Guy said as he rocked back and clasped his hands. "If you don't mind me talking a bit...?"

"I've said enough." Mike was tight lipped and drummed the rocker arm.

"Most people sell their souls chasing success. They think the busier they are the more successful they'll be. Actually, it's the opposite that works; few people can define success. So, they create more clutter and feed a culture of bad habits to support an imaginary and destructive lifestyle. They loose focus and purpose. What was it they wanted to do? They can't remember until retirement gives them the luxury of time. Then it's too late."

Mike saw himself in a rocker in his cubicle as Mr. Big passed folders through fuzzy bars as Ben tossed a racquetball. He shook his head.

5 a.m. & Already Behind

"Imagine this was your job today," Guy stood and pointed. "If this farmer had the clutter and habits most people have he'd never plow that field. He knows if he doesn't do this now, today, he won't have a crop, and if he doesn't have a crop then...." Guy eased back into the rocker.

Mike imagined himself on the porch, laughing and listening to the farmer spin tales of corn and pigs and life on the farm. He drummed faster.

"You see Mike, this farmer is disciplined, he's focused on doing the most important task he has to do; there's no busy work taking from his day. His Bahbit, if there is one, is in the barn. The mundane and monotonous are a prerequisite to his reward; that's called...all this," Guy waved his arms. "It's called the 'life he wanted'."

Mike flashed back to his father sweating and laughing and swearing as they tossed hay bales onto a slatted truck.

"And that brings us to the next assignment; you don't need your workbook, just listen. Some people have trouble with Assignment Five because it forces them to take a look at the only time they have, their day. Right now your days are filled with clutter and driven by bad habits. Understand, 'today' is only time you can take action to change your path, to fight the Bahbit. This one will make you think."

Mike opened the workbook anyway.

"You can see you have two weeks of pages, including weekends." Guy pointed to a page. "Each one is broken into hours; it's important to show the difference of what you do on work days and weekends, or other days off."

Mike puckered. "Hmmm, your right, this could be tough."

"Work hard on this one," Guy eased back. "There's a lot of insight in the details; you'll be surprised at the gap between what you think you're doing and what's actually happening."

Mike crossed his legs and closed his eyes. A breeze brought the hum of a tractor as it plowed another perfect line.

ASSIGNMENT NUMBER FOUR

1 Use your bonus workbook, or make a page as described below, which is to be used for fourteen days.

    a.   Divide each page into four columns and twenty-five rows.

    b.   Label each column as follows

        i.   *Time of day*

        ii.   *What am I doing*

        iii. *My thoughts*

        iv. *Habit*

    c.   In column one place the hour of the day beginning with 5 AM until you have completed all twenty-four hours.

2 Beginning on the first day of your assignment, complete the rows which correspond to each hour of the day as follows:

a. Column 2: Write what you do during that hour; include multiple activities if necessary.

    i. Example: *Getting ready for work*

b. Column 3: Write what you are thinking or feeling during that hour.

    i. Example: *Anxious because I'm late*

c. Column 4: Choosing from the habits you listed in Assignment Two, place those that may correspond to that hour. That includes good, bad, and should habits.

    i. Example: *Sleep too late*

    ii. *Should set my alarm and stop watching TV so late*

    iii. *Never late for work*

3 After each habit place its type in parenthesis as follows:

- **(B)** = Bad habit

- **(G)** = Good Habit

- **(S)** = Should Habit

Example:

a. *Sleep too late* **(B)**

b. *Should set my alarm and stop watching TV so late* **(S)**

C. *Never late for work* **(G)**

 At the bottom of column four total the number of *types* of each habit for that day:

Example:

- **(G)** — *2*
- **(B)** — *5*
- **(S)** — *1*

CHAPTER 6
The Top Habits

CHAPTER 6
The Top Habits

Mike peered through the steamed window of Harvey's Donut Shop. It was 5:30AM on a misty Wednesday morning in Mid-Town.

"Look who's early," Guy yelled as he appeared through the exhaust of a municipal bus. He wore a trench coat and fedora.

"Isn't there saying a about the early bird... or is it the early habit?" Mike called back.

"Yeah," Guy laughed, "he gets the freshest donut."

The shop was warm and bright with bench tables at angles to full glass windows facing an intersection.

"How are you, Harvey?" Guy yelled as he stretched over the counter.

"Hey Guy, where've you been. It's been months." Wiping his hands, Harvey ambled over, his head was shiny. "If all my customers were thin like you, I'd go broke."

"Well, I'm here today and I brought Mike; he'll make up for the last couple months."

Mike reached across the counter. Harvey's hand was pudgy and warm, like a muffin.

"I'm a two donut man," Mike patted his stomach," too many donuts already."

"Good luck, I've never met a man who could eat just one," Harvey nodded toward the rack. "Have a seat; I'll bring you something special."

They absorbed the aroma of coffee and baked bread as Harvey kept his promise. Mike was hungry; the glazed donut was hot.

"How have you been?" Guy's voice was leading.

"Actually, these past two weeks were a couple of the best weeks I've had this year."

"Why is that?" Guy's expression was unchanged, he knew the answer.

"It was like spying on... me. I rode a cloud and watched myself doing my best to waste time at things that didn't matter." Mike shrugged as glanced at the intersection: green to red. "They just didn't matter."

"Because...?"

5 a.m. & **Already Behind**

"Because, I learned days aren't forty hours long and life is short."

"Could you see the habits you wrote in Assignment Three?"

"Oh yeah, maybe better if it weren't for the smoke."

"Smoke..?"

"From all the clutter fires, that's all I did, sit in my cubicle cage and put out clutter fires. My schedule was a joke, my life is a joke. What am I doing?" Mike rubbed his eyes.

Sunrise lit the window. "Maybe it's time to do something different?"

Mike turned his workbook toward Guy, "I thought you'd never ask."

Guy slowly closed the notebook, "Let's talk about your discovery."

Mike's donut was half eaten.

"You've discovered that dreams and opportunities get buried in the clutter created by habits we add to survive a lifeless journey. Ambition morphs to struggle and clarity is replaced by exhaustion and a merry-go-round. Suddenly, your greatest challenge is seventy-five candles.

Guy cupped his hands and yelled, "Hey Harvey..."

"Yeah, Guy...?"

"What time do you close the shop?"

"I'm done at noon."

Mike sensed a charade.

"What do you do after that?"

"That's my secret; you'll never know... you'll never guess." He chuckled and backed through the kitchen door. "Never in a million years."

"O.K. Guy, the lifesaver is...?" Mike was direct.

"It starts in Assignment Five. Mike, Harvey has the will and grit to dictate his days, not the other way around. Here's where it all begins, we start clearing your clutter from the bottom up.

"From the bottom up...?"

"You'll see how it works. Turn to Assignment Two and study the habits you've written."

Mike scanned the list. "Yep, still there."

"Over the next two weeks I want you to review this list, take some walks, and ride your cloud. It's time to find out who's under the clutter.

5 a.m. & Already Behind

Mike's expression showed struggle.

"In each of the Assignment Two areas, I want you to circle the one habit, I repeat, the one habit, in each of those areas you think if changed, or added, would have the greatest immediate impact on your life... and ultimately your future. Then follow the directions for Assignment Five.

"Oh, this is gonna be easy." Mike dropped his head.

"No, it won't," Guy whispered. "But neither are your days."

ASSIGNMENT NUMBER FIVE

1 Review and reflect on the walks taken in Assignments Three and Four.

2 Using the Chapter Two assignment, "A Walk through Your Day," circle the one habit in each life area which best meets the following criteria:

    a. A bad or should habit which is used most frequently each day.

    b. A bad or should habit which you believe, if changed, removed, or added to your daily regimen will give the greatest *immediate* impact on your life.

3 Once you have circled one habit for each area, copy that habit into your bonus workbook on column two of Assignment Five marked "Most Important Bad or Should Habit." (Don't forget to add the same unique areas as those added in Assignment Two.)

4 Next, on the Assignment Five sheet, in the space provided in column four "What would change if I [Changed, Added Quit]," write what you believe would happen to each day if you changed, added, or stopped that specific habit. How would your day and life change?

5 Now, while reflecting on what you have written in column four, prioritize each habit starting at #1 and answering this question:

> **Which habit is creating the most clutter and driving my life *right now, today*?**

(Remember, this does not have to be perfect, you can always go back and change what you have written. It's your life!)

CHAPTER 7
The Bahbit

CHAPTER 7
The Bahbit

Mike handed his ticket to an attendant wearing a blue uniform. The midday was clear and warm, the zoo filled with tourists and children. He remembered his father throwing birdseed and scuffing down dirt paths to growl at the bears. Flowers, red, lined new sidewalks as clowns waved twisted balloons.

"Hey Mike," Guy yelled from a concrete table shaded by a striped umbrella.

A round man wearing khakis and safari hat straddled the bench next to Guy.

As Mike approached, Guy stood and threw out his arm and announced, "Meet Marko... tamer of the lions."

"Oh that was great, Guy," the round man blushed. "Hi Mike, I'm Mark and I feed the lions. Sometimes Guy has a little fantasy thing." He pushed up from the table.

"I've sensed that about him."

"Listen Mike, have fun with Guy and all the other animals, it's time to feed the ladies." Mark squeezed Mike's hand and sauntered into the crowd.

"Let's take a walk." Guy was like a kid.

They strolled without talking, Mike watched the fathers point and teach. "It really hasn't changed much," he thought. They stopped in front of a cage filled with a tree bunched with busy Rhesus monkeys.

"What do you think they're thinking?" Guy shaded his eyes.

"They're wondering why we all look the same but try to be different. They're laughing at us; I remember what my father and I used to do in front of these cages." He touched the bar, "Now that was fun."

"And now...?" Guy glanced at Mike.

"The answer is obvious. Life isn't fun; my days aren't fun, and even if I wanted to have fun it'd have to be forced into my useless schedule. I can hear my psyche telling me, 'you must find fun'..." He made a chewing sound, "Yep, fun, fun, fun..."

"Tell me about the last two weeks." Guy glanced at the workbook Mike was tapping against his jeans.

"It was a search and rescue mission."

"Really..?"

"Yeah, I relived my walks and studied my habits and went back and forth for the first week; I couldn't settle on six. Finally, on Sunday morning I camped at the kitchen table and stared at the book; I had to get it done. Then they jumped, within five minutes the six habits were circled; I felt like I'd finished a marathon."

"What did you do the rest of the week?"

"I took ten minutes every morning and updated my clutter list, but it was different. This time, the clutter associated with those six habits lit up like stars. I just laughed, it was so obvious."

"What you saw Mike, was the cause of anxiety and poverty and heart disease," Guy paused, "and the great intangible: unhappiness."

Mike imagined his doctor checking off a list and repeating, "Uh huh."

Guy turned and pointed to the tree. "These guys are smarter than we are, they don't waste today cleaning up the clutter from yesterday. They focus every blink on survival; there is no tomorrow if a lion catches them daydreaming."

The monkeys stared; Mike saw Mrs. Chestnut, his first grade teacher.

"The next two weeks are 'weeks of preparation'," Guy's voice was fatherly. "In Assignment Six, you're going to pick one of the six habits you circled. That habit will become our focus, your focus."

"I had a feeling that's where we were going," Mike licked his lips. "They all stand out, how do I pick the Bahbit? How do I know that's the one?"

Guy clapped his hands and laughed. "Mike, my friend, ask your clutter."

5 a.m. & Already Behind

ASSIGNMENT NUMBER SIX

1 Plan a quiet time to reread your bonus workbook or workbook pages you have created, and think about the habits you have written in Assignment Five.

2 Now, turn to Assignment Five and circle the *one habit* that best answers the questions below. *(Hint: It may not be the one you prioritized as #1)*

   a.   Which habit will have the greatest impact on my life — immediately?

   b.   Which habit will have the greatest long term affect on my life?

   c.   Which habit will help me get rid of the clutter?

   d.   Which habit will help me lead a happier life?

   e.   Which habit is holding me back?

   f.   Which habit can I change: *Now*

3 Congratulations! You have just identified your "Bahbit."

4 After circling your one habit (Bahbit), write it in the space provided at the top of the page for Assignment Six: "*My Bahbit Is.*"

5 In the space provided for Assignment Six write what would happen in each of the areas of your life if you [Changed, Added, or Quit] that Bahbit *today*. (Don't forget to add your unique life areas as you had done previously).

CHAPTER 8
Excuses

CHAPTER 8
Excuses

Mike eased along the mountain road. It was 10 PM. "Maybe Guy is crazy," he muttered. Heights made him queasy.

The road ended in a parking lot darkened by redwood silhouettes. A path of yellow lights crisscrossed to a dome outlined above the tree line. "So this is Guy's surprise," Mike whispered as he began the climb, "an observatory."

"I hope that's you Mike."

"Real funny, Guy..." Mike sagged on the top platform, hands on his knees. "My wife asked where I was going and all I could say was 'I'm not sure'." His breathing slowed, "and ...I don't like heights."

Sorry about the climb, but I thought you'd like to see a one-of-kind show," Guy cracked his knuckles, "the real 'Greatest Show on Earth'." He directed Mike toward a door marked Employees Only, "What do you know about astronomy?"

Mike stopped and gazed at the moonless sky. "I can find the two Dippers, but that's about it."

"Well Mike, there might be a few more; you'll see."

The domed ceiling of the empty auditorium was bathed in amber. Seats faced a lectern in front of a door: Control Room.

A voice echoed from the dome, "What an odd place for a Saturday night date."

Guy yelled through cupped hands, "Where else would I rather be, eating pizza, having a cold beer, listening to you ramble about science projects?"

A man leaned from the Control Room, "But I won the science fair and beat you didn't I?"

Guy pressed a finger to his temple. "Yes, I seem to remember...you did that more than once, no, every single time." They hugged and turned to Mike.

"Mike, I'd like you to meet Jerry. He's my best friend." Jerry's grasp was wide with tentacle fingers; his eyes, intelligent and warm.

"We grew up together," Guy crooked smiled at Jerry. "Yep, same neighborhood, same schools, and even tried the same girl friend."

5 **a.m. & Already Behind**

"Fifth grade," Jerry raised thin eyebrows. "Neither one of us won that one."

"In real life," Guy continued, "he's a meteorologist, an astronomer, and a few other things. I think he has a surprise for us."

"Yes, I do," Jerry rolled his hands. "Have a seat in the middle; it's the best spot. I'll be back out after I start the show. It's automated, but on special occasions I like to add flavor." Winking, he vanished into the control room.

A screen descended and a movie explained the observatory and how stars would be projected in real-time from a telescope mounted above the auditorium.

"This is fascinating." Mike thought of popcorn.

The film ended and the room went black; Jerry slid in next to Mike.

"I never get tired of this."

Mike held his breath as the dome became God's masterpiece. The creation demanded emotion.

A voice told of galaxies, planets, stars, and life. With each inference, stars would brighten and their name, in orange, would fade in and out. Jerry used a laser light.

"That one's a meteor; he's been trying to pass us for two million years."

Thirty minutes passed in seconds and the stars faded to amber.

Jerry stood, bowed, and touched Mike's shoulder. "Good luck to you Mike, and remember," gesturing to the dome, "nothing is impossible."

Mike remained still. He thought of church and sermons and his family and the farm. The room was soundless; they stared at the dome.

"You win."

"Sometimes... it's not about winning."

"I used to know that."

"Did you find your Bahbit?"

"I've circled it." Mike squirmed, "Do you want to know which one?"

"Not now, that's your secret; it's your life. Let's talk about the stars and Assignment Seven."

Mike fought impatience but the tone of Guy's voice suggested there was something else, something more than a trip to the stars.

"We all have great plans; I know you're anxious to get started, but there's an issue you must deal with first." He scooted forward and faced Mike, "Your excuses."

"Ah yes, my excuses..." Mike winced; a sigh escaped.

"Excuses are like the solar system, endless. You need focus to clear your clutter. Excuses will blur your vision and its brother, procrastination, will extinguish the resolve to make permanent change. The Bahbit you circled will end up another 'I meant to do' and float off," Guy wagged his hand, "into space."

Mike's mind danced; his subconscious wanted to yank him into next week.

Guy was stern. "For the next two weeks I want you to think of the stars and write every excuse, every barrier, and every reason you can see or think of that will stop you from changing that Bahbit." He tapped Mike's arm, "every single one."

Mike imagined a twinkling dome over his cubicle. "At least...I can count the stars."

ASSIGNMENT NUMBER SEVEN

1 Turn to Assignment Seven in your bonus workbook:

    a.   Write your Bahbit in the area at the top of the page; "My Bahbit Is."

    b.   Using the numbered areas, or free writing on the page provided, look at your Bahbit and answer this question:

> **What is stopping me from [changing, adding, or quitting] my Bahbit: Tomorrow?**

2 Repeat this process for two weeks, adding excuses each day until you can add no more.

CHAPTER 9
Plans

CHAPTER 9
Plans

The construction site was hazed in afternoon dust. Mike sipped coffee and watched yellow monsters shape clay mountains as dump trucks waited to add to their load. A river split the site; Mike guessed a bridge and maybe another mall. He jumped at the knock on the window.

Guy wore jeans and a tee shirt, his face was shaded by a construction hat.

"You'll need these." Guy handed him a yellow hard-hat and coveralls, "Your shoes may get a little dirty."

Mike leaned against the car and struggled with the coveralls. He adjusted the hard hat then stepped out and turned, hands out and palms up. "How's that, I'm a construction person."

"Not bad; I know somebody who'd love to give you a job."

They walked toward a trailer that looked like a shoebox. Guy rapped once then entered. A burly man stood from a desk blanketed in blueprints, "You must be Mike."

Mike nodded as his soft hand was engulfed in a calloused handshake.

"Mike, this is Mory. He's the engineer running this whole shebang."

"Or it's running me," Mory snorted. "Guy tells me you want to drive one of those dozers."

"What?" Mike's mouth opened as Guy lifted one eyebrow. "I drive a car and a bike; I've never been close to one of those things."

"There are a lot of things you haven't done." Guy thumped Mike's arm. "Sometimes you've got to have faith, take a little risk. It'll be, let's say, today's challenge."

Mike jiggled as the pick-up bumped across the site to a fenced area filled with machines. Mory pointed to a bull-dozer outside the perimeter and announced, "There she is."

"You're serious?" Mike's expression was pleading.

"Dead serious," Guy turned to Mike. "There are a lot of things you never get to do in life. After today, you can check this one off the list."

5 a.m. & Already Behind

"This wasn't on my list."

"It is now, come on."

Mory climbed onto the machine and motioned. Mike hesitated, glanced at Guy, then grabbed two metal handles and pulled himself into the seat.

Guy yelled, "You look good, a natural: forget the day job." He was laughing.

Mory reviewed the levers. "You can't hurt anything out here, but these won't float, so stay away from the river."

"That's funny Mory." Mike stared forward, "Let's get this over with."

"I'll just sit back here and tell you what to do. Remember this ain't a car; you steer with your feet."

"I got it." Mike's pulse pounded.

"Let's get it then, crank her up."

The animal came alive; diesel smoke turned Mike's fear into focus.

"Move that lever," Mory yelled. The machine coughed and lurched and for an hour it circled and pushed dirt into long piles. Finally, Mike hit the red button and turned to Mory. He was already gone; Mike hadn't noticed.

"Just leave the lights on when you leave. I want people to think somebody's in here." They watched Mory leave and the trailer was quiet.

"I could have killed myself. What would you have told my wife?" Mike said as he washed his hands.

"That you were just having fun," Guy waved a water bottle. "So, do you have the list?"

"List?" feigning memory loss. He pointed, "It's on the counter."

"How did it go?"

"It was like weeding a garden, new excuses popped up every day. I can't imagine trying to change two habits at the same time.

"Are any of them true?" Guy asked.

"True?"

"Do you really think they're valid? Will the excuse weeds choke you into mediocrity?" Guys question ended with an upturn.

Mike flicked his tongue. "No, not if I want to make this work, not if I want to be happy."

5 a.m. & Already Behind

"Open your notebook to the excuse list." He tossed Mike a drawing pencil.

Mike placed the workbook on the blueprints, "There they are."

"Just put an X across this page."

Mike twiddled.

"Excuses are the blight of purpose." Guy snapped his fingers, touched the page and said slowly, "These are not real."

Mike dragged the pencil from corner to corner. "Now, that felt good"

"Mike, why do you think you're here today?"

"I know it wasn't just the bulldozer."

"Do you think they can build this bridge without a plan? Look at these."

Mike stared at perfect angles and squiggles.

"It's all about the plan."

Mike listened; it was a long day.

"The bridges over the clutter in your life can't be built on a wish; they need a blueprint. How scared were you when you climbed on that bulldozer?' Guy clapped, "You drove a bulldozer and had the time of your life, actual fun. The next two weeks is about your blueprint to a new life. You don't have any excuses, right?"

Mike nodded.

"Excuses gone; plan in place. That's where we're going in Assignment Eight, you get a chance to run the show, to plan your new life without clutter and barriers and the Bahbit that's been holding you down."

Mike's face was streaked. "Yep," he said, "that's where we're going,"

5 a.m. & **Already Behind**

ASSIGNMENT NUMBER EIGHT

1 Turn to the page in the workbook marked Assignment Eight. "Plans" is written on top of the page.

2 Write your Bahbit in the space provided: "My Bahbit Is."

3 In the numbered spaces below you will form a list by answering this question:

    a.   What would I have to do *today* in order to be ready to {change, add, or quit} my Bahbit: *Tomorrow*?

    b.   Continue answering this question daily for the next two weeks until your list is complete.

4 Some helpful questions you may ask are:

    ● How much money do I need?

- What do I have to buy?

- What schedule do I have to change, or rearrange?

- Who do I have to call?

- Who has the expertise to help me?

- What else do I have to know?

- Who do I know that will hold me accountable?

CHAPTER 10

Contract with Yourself

CHAPTER 10
Contract with Yourself

Traffic was extreme on Friday afternoon. "I should have taken a taxi," Mike mumbled. The meeting was scheduled for 5 P.M. in the Glazer Building. It was 4:35 P.M. and another mile to go. At this pace, he thought, I might get there in an hour.

Two minutes yielded a half block; Mike felt neck pressure. "Don't get mad," his grip tighter, "just figure it out; get a plan, get a plan..." He spied a parking garage entrance ten yards away. "That's the plan." He pulled a ticket from the automated attendant, whipped into the first space, grabbed his workbook, and jogged down the sidewalk.

Mike read a gold plate on the double door, "Billings and Billings, Attorneys at Law". He wiped his forehead and walked into a bright lobby decorated in royal blue and oak. "Now what," he thought as he was met by a perfect secretary. The sweat gave him away.

"You must be Mr. Lamb. Please sit down; I'll get you some water." She returned with a cold bottle and handed him a manila folder.

"Guy is in the back. He asked that you review this before your meeting." Her smile was tight but not fake.

Mike thanked her as he pulled a black spiral notebook from the folder, the front was blank. He read the first page, "Contract for Sale," and then scanned the others.

"Did you get that read?" Guy was crossing the room. "Sheila said you looked flushed."

"Just a little exercise program I invented," Mike said, getting his humor back."I call it the one mile parking lot dash."

"Let's go where it's cooler." Guy gestured. They entered an office; it was spacious and uncluttered with wood floors and Persian rugs.

"Don't act so busy," Guy said to the back of a blue leather chair. The chair swiveled and a small man jumped out, extended his arms and yelled "Hey, hey, hey." He was dressed in a sweat suit and jogged around the desk.

"Never too busy for you, Guy," shaking Guy's shoulders. He turned to Mike and dropped his arms to a hand-

shake, "No hugs on the first date." His grasp was small and firm, "But, I already know you."

Mike was confused, "You know me?"

"Well, I know about you because you're with Guy." Terry leaned against the desk. "I have known him a long time," he said, raising a finger "and I know you have no idea what I'm talking about." He grinned at Guy. "Hey, I just wanted to tell Mike he's lucky to have you as a friend."

Guy took three steps then pivoted. "Terry and I started college together, he wanted to go to law school and I wanted to be a doctor. Our families were poor." They looked at each other as old friends. "Everyone told us we were dreamers; it would never happen. They were wrong."

"You're a doctor?" Mike half turned to Guy, face contorted, "A doctor?"

"And a great one at that..." Terry beamed, pointing his hand like a gun.

"Anyway," Guy continued as if nothing was said, "here we are in this dreamer's office and as you can see," Guy waved one hand to the room, "he's quite successful... except for his clothes."

"Hey, it's Friday— I meet my wife at the gym and then a few Martinis...and I'm already late." He snapped a briefcase and walked toward the door. "It's a great life. Yep, just another dreamer. It was great meeting you, Mike."

"Have a seat," Guy motioned. "Mike, I know you want to ask, but today's not about me, it's about you, your clutter, your habits and," pausing to take the contract notebook from Mike, "about contracts."

Contracts...?"

"Terry is one of the best contract attorneys in the country," Guy explained. "If he draws up a contract, you'd better believe it's air tight." Guy raised the contract book. "This represents our commitment to do what we promise; to hold us accountable. Cluttered and unfocused lives allow people to slip out of commitments that could lead to a new day and a new life. Imagine where you'd be if you had kept every promise you ever made...every promise to yourself?

Mike didn't answer. He saw his high school graduation and his mother crying.

"Do you have your plan?"

Mike mini-jerked and stood straight. He exhaled, "Yeah, I have a plan," then louder, "I think it's a good plan."

5 a.m. & Already Behind

"And you can start your habit change tomorrow?"

Reality was Mike's expression. He hesitated, "Yes, tomorrow. That's my plan; really...tomorrow." Good grief, Mike thought, this is really going to happen... tomorrow.

"Then let's sign the contract."

"Sign the contract?"

"Sign the Contract..." Guy opened Mike's workbook and tapped it with a pen.

Mike read out loud, "A contract with yourself, hmmm." Taking the pen, he bent and cocked his head. "So, this is it?"

"This is it." Guy didn't blink.

Mike filled the blanks and hesitated at the last line.

"We never break a contract," Guy staccatoed and touched Mike's shoulder.

Mike stared at his signature and repeated, "We never break a contract."

ASSIGNMENT NUMBER NINE

1 In your bonus workbook, fill in the blanks of your contract using your Bahbit.

2 Note:

    a.   The contract requires that the habit you have chosen to {change, add, or quit} *must begin tomorrow.*

    b.   This Bahbit change must take place per the regimen as defined on the contract for a *continuous six months.*

CHAPTER 11
Six Months Later

CHAPTER 11
Six Months Later

"**M**r. Lamb," the chef announced, "welcome back." He pumped Mike's hand and guided him between tables. "Look who I found," his Italian exaggerated.

Guy waved a glass of Merlot. "Do I know you?" He closed one eye.

"My name's Mike, Mike Lamb. I believe I'm ten minutes early."

Guy slowly gazed at Mike's shoes, gloss black, and then moved all the way up to his cropped hair. He was tanned, his face thin and confident.

"You look the same to me." Guy smiled. "Nope, nothing new here."

Guy's pride filled the silence as he squeezed Mike's hand.

"Please, Mike, sit down and tell me how you did it." Guy gestured to the chair.

"I just did it. I did what you said; I just changed one thing, one Bahbit." He paused and waved a finger, "Oh, and the job, too. So, I changed one Bahbit and the job really had to go, that's it; that's all. The rest just fell in place."

"And the clutter..?" Guy asked.

"Once it cleared I could see I'd been living in the land of no purpose." His voice softened. "That had to stop. That had to change. I never understood how much clutter one Bahbit could create until it was gone." Mike chose his words, "Guy, you were right. I discovered secrets and dreams and emotions; I have a new life. And one other thing..."

Guy sat quietly.

"What I changed affected everything else, all the other habits. You know what I mean? All the habits supported each other and when I removed the Bahbit, the big pyramid block, the others began to crumble. It was amazing, I had control."

"How much weight have you lost?" Guy focused.

"All I needed, and a few pounds for the heck of it," Mike flexed. "I'm back in football shape again. I feel great, I look great, and most of all," he whispered, "I sleep at night."

Guy listened. He knew Mike had more to say; they all did.

5 a.m. & Already Behind

"Guy," he announced, "I stuck to my contract, and today I fill out my second one. There's still some clutter, but I know I can get rid of it. What's more important is I know how to prevent it. I'll never get buried again, that's a promise to you, me... and my wife."

"Mike," Guy was serious, "look around the room."

The restaurant was half full: couples, candles, and wine. Mike's eye's narrowed, "Wait a minute." He stood slowly and whispered, "very funny."

On one table lay a hard hat next to a plate of donuts. He recognized the smile of a country waitress while a tall man waved a star on a stick. Marty backed from the kitchen with a cake and six sparkler candles. Mike's eyes moistened; he swayed as they eased to his table.

"Mike, I'd like you to meet my students."

"Your students...?"

Guy pointed, "Linda the librarian gave up her cluttered life as a corporate CEO for the love of quiet and books. Sometimes people misunderstand what drives success. It was never power she sought, just a chance to live and learn lessons from two thousand years of great writers.

"Harry over there," Harry tipped his striped hat, "could have stayed a successful industrial engineer, but he never wanted to grow up. Now he's discovered what it's like to live his boyhood dream." Guy grinned, "He just got his engineers mixed up."

"And...the life of a French chef was eating away at Harvey's need for simplicity and freedom, pardon the pun, and although it's not fancy, he does make the best gourmet donuts in town." Harvey smiled and Mike understood.

"And Mark," Guy gave a 'thumbs up', "was never much for people and his job at the accounting firm. He loved animals, big animals. So, he found a place to live his passion, every day of his life."

"Ah yes, the farm life for Betty..." She curtseyed and glowed in a puffy dress. "Her days as a flight attendant were too fast. Oh Mike, some day I'll tell you a love story about a girl who discovered the life she was chasing was nothing but clutter and fiction."

"Jerry, my lifelong friend, came to me three years ago," Jerry leaned an elbow on Guy's shoulder. "His star fantasy and need to teach just weren't being fulfilled at the space center; he needed an uncluttered place without mental restriction. Someday, he may just change this world." Guy scanned the room and waved.

"The architect in Mory was no match for dust and draglines. Being inside and wearing a tie built clutter and kept him from seeing and living his imagination. He needed to be in the dust, actually building the ideas he learned to create and draw."

"And then there's Terry." Guy tilted his head and gazed up at the attorney. "He's discovered that purpose must be built on the ethics and principles that serve people, it's never about us. Guy lifted his glass, "Once an attorney... always an attorney." They all laughed.

"So Mike," the room was quiet," welcome to a most elite group; people who chose meaning over a life of clutter." Guy winked as he placed his hand on Mike's arm, "I hope someday, I can share your story with another Mike."

"You bet, Guy," Mike cleared his throat. "Anytime..."

 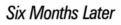

ASSIGNMENT NUMBER TEN
Your New Contract

1 Look back through your workbook and Assignment Five and pick the next Bahbit that if [changed, added, or removed] will most impact your new life.

2 Note that with the changes you've made, the new Bahbit may not be the one listed in as the next priority in Assignment Five. It may not be listed at all, and you may have to add it!

3 Go through Assignments Six through Assignment Eight with the new Bahbit.

4 Sign a new contract in Assignment Nine.

5 Repeat this process every six months until your Bahbits are gone and you are in control of your life.

IMAGINE

Imagine. Imagine you're eighty years old and sitting in my office and telling your story. You talk about your life and your family and the friends that have passed. You think back on a day you read a book and took a chance to make a change. When you look back you realize that single effort, early in your life, made all the difference. It did matter.

~Dr. D.E. Kennedy

ABOUT DR. DON KENNEDY, MBA

Donald E. Kennedy is a respected authority in family medicine and disease prevention with special interests in the neuroscience of change, leadership, and the habits that drive our lives. He is a family physician, author, professional speaker, teacher, and business consultant who teaches the lessons and principles of self-direction and personal change taken from over twenty five years of patient stories and care.

Dr. Kennedy is a Diplomat of the American College of Family Medicine, holds a Masters in Business Administration degree from Stetson University, and teaches as an Assistant Clinical Professor for the Lake Erie College of Osteopathic Medicine. He continues to practice family and geriatric medicine and is an active member of the National Speakers Association as well as a certified coach and facilitator. Dr. Kennedy has spoken for companies such as Merck, Schering-Plough, Younglife, Rotary International, and Pfizer.

Raised in poverty as the son of a professional bull-rider, Dr. Kennedy's story is a remarkable testimonial to the will-power of personal change. Dr. Kennedy is now the father of four and grandfather of two. He is the Co-founder of Murdock Family Medicine and the founder and CEO of Kennedy Consulting, LLC and Bahbit, LLC.

For further information on speaking engagements, seminars, books, and upcoming events please visit:

www.bahbits.com

5 **a.m. & Already Behind**

FREE BONUS POWER OF AN HOUR AUDIO INTERVIEW

FREE Audio Recording
with Dr. Don Kennedy, MBA
and Dave Lakhani, author of "Power of an Hour"

"WAKE-UP!"
3 Steps to Telling the Story You were Created to Tell

It's 5 A.M., and you're already behind. You're tired, and every day you mold looks just like the others. It's time to change something, but you don't know what, or how, or where to begin.

The truth is: Most people never do make the change. They ease into retirement and say "I wish I had…". But that's not you!

Listen as Dave Lakhani, author of "Power of an Hour", interviews Dr. Kennedy about his remarkable story and the three steps he's used to help thousands of patients and clients mold a different day and live a new story.

DOWNLOAD RECORDING AT:
www.Its5am.com/5ambookbonus

Printed in the United States
201106BV00002B/244-525/A

9 781600 373442